SIGNS
AND
WONDERS

Poems by
Carl Dennis

Princeton University Press
Princeton, New Jersey

Publication of this book has been aided by a grant from the Paul
Mellon Fund of Princeton University Press

This book has been composed in VIP Bembo

Clothbound editions of Princeton University Press books are
printed on acid-free paper, and binding materials are chosen for
strength and durability

Printed in the United States of America by Princeton
University Press, Princeton, New Jersey

For my mother, Fay Dennis,
and in memory of my father, Israel Dennis

By Carl Dennis

A House of My Own (1974)
Climbing Down (1976)

Acknowledgments

Thanks are due to the editors of the magazines in which the following poems first appeared:

American Poetry Review, "Oyez! Oyez!";

The Blue Guitar (Messina), Vol. 2 (1976), "Late Work," "The Traitor," "Everywhere," "The Blind Man," and "Sunday";

Choice 10, "Contentment";

Concerning Poetry, "Carpentry" and "The Trip";

Epoch, "Morning" (Spring 1975) and "Margaret's Answer" (Fall 1977);

The Laurel Review, Vol. 12, No. 1, "Near Idaville," originally published as "The Happy Few";

Modern Poetry Studies, "The Pilgrims";

The New England Review, Vol. 1, No. 2 (Winter 1978), "Over There";

The New Yorker, "Snow" (p. 5), © 1975 The New Yorker Magazine Inc.; "Signs" (p. 15), © 1977 The New Yorker Magazine Inc.;

Poetry Northwest, Vol. 16, No. 3 (Autumn 1975), "My Brother's House," © 1975 University of Washington; (Summer 1979), "Evening Guide," originally published as "Backyard Guidebook," "Fiction," "Igor," "The Reunion," and "Where Have You Been?";

Salmagundi, Nos. 28 (Winter 1975), "Early Photograph"; 31-32 (Fall 1975-Winter 1976), "Early Settler"; 35 (Fall 1976), "Ashland Avenue"; 38-39 (Summer-Fall 1977), "Grandmother and I";

The South Dakota Review, "The Tree" and "Today";

The Virginia Quarterly Review (Summer 1979), "The Band" and "In the West."

"Ithaka" was first published as a Christmas Broadside by the Lockwood Library of the State University of New York at Buffalo. Some of the details of "Masonry" were suggested by an interview with a mason in Studs Terkel's *Working* (New York, 1974).

Contents

I *Quiet Neighbors*

Listeners

After midnight, when I phone up a far-off friend
To describe my chills or a blister by the heart
That won't wait, I can hear the breath of the operator
As she listens in, lonely among the night wires.
They all do it, breaking the rules.
In the morning she takes home my story to her
        husband, her friends.
A sad burden. No useful wisdom yet.
No advice about selling the house, the move to Florida,
The right neighborhood for the boys.

It's getting harder to tell where the words go.
You send them off with instructions not to stop on the
        road,
Not to speak to strangers, but as they run they spill
        over.
Even on a bare bench when you whisper to yourself,
Sigh softly how the world has let you down,
From the bench in back you can hear a breath.
Your thoughts have entered the far world;
They have changed to stones,
And someone walks round them as he climbs.

My Brother's House

Dinner isn't ready in my brother's house.
The babies upstairs hammer their heads
On the loose bars of the crib.

In the livingroom, the piano, tuned only last week,
Waits for my brother's fingers,
While the fingers themselves, mindless,
Would be just as happy tearing orange peels
Or digging for clams, unconcerned
Should my brother's skills melt away
Like snow in the swamps.

In the quiet interval after dinner
He sits on the couch trying to recall a friend.
Now she lives on only in him,
And though her face looks young still and calm,
Even in his dream she can't speak any more or sing.
So he can't tell if she's pleased
When he sits all evening with an art book
And stares at the painted trees
And the coastlines she might have considered beautiful.

As he sits there he hums to himself a tune
He's not aware of, composed in his sleep,
Drifting up to the mind's edge
With no name, a formless song
Like the sound muttered by giraffes
To the tender leaf tops,
Or the music of turtles singing in the wilderness,
Drifting over the trees unheard
To the distant hush and wash of the sea.

Snow

Thirty-four years haven't put a dent
In my vision of snowstorms, my impatience
With the paltry inches of the winter dole,
Slim pickings even in Buffalo.
My hunger is to wake in the morning
In the deep dark, the windows snowed over,
The doors opening into walls. No one can move.
Nothing to do but tunnel. So I push out
With my snow shovel, clearing a dark hall
To the buried tool shed, quieting my rabbits
And spaniels, who feed from my hand.
Then I rescue my neighbor, tunnel through the town,
Stopping to relieve the drugstore, helping the weeping
    pharmacist
From behind the counter. He offers me
Medicine for a lifetime, which I refuse.
I dig to uncover roofs and porches.
At every door I leave frozen breadloaves,
Pound with stone fists and hurry away,
Too busy to wait for an introduction.
The hungry families spend hours in vain
Guessing the name of their deliverer.

Oyez! Oyez!

Her boyfriend wrote her every week from France;
But when the war was over, and the boys came home,
He changed his plans, and never returned to Beeber
        Crossing.
His final letter, friendly and honest, froze her heart.
She didn't thaw out that spring when the rivers did,
Or all that summer, or summers beyond,
Though other girls got over their letters in a month
Of crying, or a year, and married the Willis boys,
And raised three children, two of whom still fly home
On the holidays. Maybe her parents neglected her,
Destroyed her confidence, or maybe by nature her heart
        was frail
Or too small, no gifts left over after the first.
But that can't be right. Every year for twenty-five years
She chipped away at the ice, through four
        Administrations,
Lukewarm Presidents, Ohio's freeze, Ohio's thaw.
When at last she dug her heart out, it must have been
        stiff,
Frosty, but still alive, young in a way,
Preserved in its cold sleep, ready to be tried.
But by then the friends she might have enjoyed were
        old.
The men who needed her help were happy with others
Or unhappy and worn down,
Insurance claim-adjusters in California,
Retired early, or fired, and for no reason,
All taking it with no complaints on the chin,

All except one, maybe, some stubborn man
Easy for her to admire, if she ever met him.
But he'd neglect her, turn from her available love
To years of pacing the courthouse, crying for justice,
Demanding that the jury return a verdict at last,
As if the arguments had been heard, as if his case,
Come round on the docket, were finally pending.

Distance

As he bends by the far-off tree, your mute neighbor,
Small at this distance as a child, his face half-shadowed,
Is still too close to be beautiful.

Only stones are always far enough.
Their moss scars, their broken cinder moles,
Are not beautiful in themselves,
But because they are never where you are,
Where your voice can reach.
Put your ear on the stone face
And you'll hear stone all the way through
For a thousand miles, keeping to itself,
Obeying undistracted with its whole weight
Its stony laws.

You would like to be beautiful like that,
Live with them far off,
If only you could bring your friends.
But who would come to you among stones?
Who would be heard when he leaned down
And shouted in the sandy cleft of your ear,
"Dear Brother, are you well?
Are you feeling strong?"

At the Hospital

On the garden bench of the hospital,
Resting behind trim hedges in the shade,
My friend looks peaceful for the first time.
"Good thoughts," he explains, "make a good life.
So I sit here all day thinking good thoughts:
How many more little threads
Reach out by evening from this bench
To tie themselves to fences and barns.
The faintest twitching of my hand,
The ghost of a wish to haul them in,
Would break each one. So I sit still,
My fingers like stone, my bench
The quiet tether of the world.

"Do you see those patients over there,
How they wedge their faces between the fence bars
To stare at the road? These are the ones
Who wake me at night with crying.
Should I make myself join in out of fellowship,
Pretending to cry so they won't feel alone?
That would be a thread from my bench to theirs.
But they, reaching out, needy and ignorant,
Would break what might have held for years."

Near Idaville

Has the story reached you of those few who live alone
And love it, and never open their mail?
The long Sahara of summer vacation is for them a sea.
They put forth boldly on the billowy mornings,
Crowd sail through fragrant nights when no one
         knocks,
Free at last for their mission to rewrite
The history of the world in a room
Near Idaville, in back of the drygoods store.
Hunched by the lamp, each asks a question of himself;
Each listens thoughtfully to his own replies.
Wiser than before, he jots them down.
In his one-man apartment a quiet pair,
A lifetime of dialogue.

How far away this life is, even from your solitude.
For always on your hunting trip to the North,
In your rented cabin, at the edge of the pines,
With a wide prospect of the valley, you hope for
         visitors,
And imagine a couple beside you sharing the view.
And they, your own creations, though they love the
         quiet,
Want visitors too, and dream of the field
Filled with strangers who look like friends, but happier,
A congenial race of enlightened souls
Walking arm in arm in graceful pairs
Slowly along the hills and down,

Greeting each other with warm ceremonious smiles.

And you imagine them too, and wait for them.
And you're sure that whoever hopes for their company
Deserves to be loved not for himself or his work
But his endless need to become like them,
These strangers who are not yet here,
Whose bones, though beautiful, though sure to endure,
Are thin as light and light as air.

The Tree

Only the outermost ring of the tree you love
Is alive. All trees are like that,
The spine wholly dead
And the dead wood undecayed,
Bracing the sap-flow just under the bark.
Slowly the sap edges up.
The moistened leaves, furled up on top,
Spring open when the daylight is long enough,
Spread to the sun
And sweeten the juice in the live rim
While the dead cores of the branches stick out.

But your core is hungry.
Listen how the tree inside
Scratches as it sways in the night wind,
Knocks its branches in the dark under the ribs.
It's hard to tell where its roots are bedded,
What clear pool it's groping for;
Hard to know if it's nourished
When you walk out under the stars
Or read late by the fire.
If it dies it dies from within,
Crumbles to nothing, and you live on
Afraid of the wind,
Branches scattered on the ground,
The hollow trunk filling up with leaves.

Margaret's Answer

Your letter spoiled everything.
How could rumors like those take you in?
I've tried so hard to be patient with the family.
Almost every night, in the few moments saved for
      myself,
I pull a book from the box you left
And read slowly, trying my best
To understand why it's good.

It's always on one of my few bad days
That your friend with the cold eyes
Drops by for dinner. He's never liked me.
Does he write that I've pulled down your picture,
Thrown out your furniture, rented your room?
He's read about politics for so long
Every tree in his neighborhood plots for power.

And who comes by on my best days?
Only Uncle Dan, too tired from his shop
To hear one word. At dinner his eyes
Focus on the food, hover at the window.
He's anxious to get home.
Rising for his coat he promises to write you soon
And mention how well I've been getting on.
Then he climbs in his truck and forgets everything.

I don't expect to convince you, and won't try,

Though I'd like to hear from you anyway.
The weather here's been good.
Every night the smallest stars are visible.
Their slow steadiness has always seemed beautiful.
Now of all their beauties I admire most
Their austere refusal to make one sign,
One little flare as they sail over.

Signs

When you go I want a clear sign,
A door shut by accident on my hand
Or a tooth broken that morning on the steering wheel
As I stop short driving to work
And taste blood in the gap.
I want to feel it all now
With simple grief rising in a wail
As you wave at me from the car.
Not a dull pain floating yards off;
Not to wake up years later,
Ease out of bed, and fall,
My legs sometime in the winter gone stiff,
The walls in the room too weak to lean on,
The floor sliding out of reach below.

The Blind Man

I didn't need this blindness to remind me.
For a long time my backbone curved to hospitals.
I'm familiar with the bone wards.
No need at all for my papers and pencils
To fall dark. Did I ever pretend
My sentences had saved anything?
Here, surely, the lesson of blindness
Has gone to waste.

Now I'm listening to the art of old men.
In Haydn's late quartets the spirit is calm,
Patient, accepting. In his final plays
Shakespeare forgives Polonius for his vanities,
Forgives the arrogance of five kings.

I should start forgiving my frightened friends.
Who can blame them for smelling death in my room?
After a chat with my blank eyes,
After rubbing alcohol on my bones,
They're called by life to the air outside,
The splendid sun. Their strong voices
Soar through the window and settle on the sheet.
Each word glints with an inch of light.
I watch them all with dark eyes as they dim
And dwindle, and die out.

Red Creek

for Charles Altieri

Climbing down to wade in Red Creek,
You lose the view, the miles of its curves
Shining like a ribbon below the hill.

Wading in from the bank you lose the fish
As they weave among bottom rocks
In clear water. At your first step
The bottom jars loose
And rises in clouds.

Cool water on cracked feet,
Water in your dry mouth,
These are the simple pleasures left
With the joy of rippling Red Creek:
The invisible rise of the surface as you wade in,
The invisible fall as you drink.

A Plea for More Time

New Year's already come and gone
And the wish still miles away
To live here again;

To be cast up after an interval
Back to this yard, the same man,
No Heaven or Hell between,

Immortal return to the lumberpile.
After sweating out new plans for a table
To build the old one again.

So little time left, and still
Nothing I have won would make me glad
To win it forever;

To notice a mirror face at the window
With lines I would weep to alter,
Like the face of a friend.

And to think of walking the night rounds
Full of love for my gatelocks,
Blessing the knots of boundary wire

And the hills behind blocking my view;
How strangely slow the watchman saunters;
How far away he seems even now.

II *The Happy Few*

Early Photograph

Hard now to imagine them,
The small couple in the picture,
Serious by the cabin door.
They peer hard through the sunlight and air,
Their bodies erect, poised for the orders
To soften the earth with sweat at the far corners
Of their dirt-farm homestead.
It's not his own wife or her own husband
Each holds here by the hand,
But the destined companion,
Fellow guardian to the children inside,
To the family they carry Sundays to the river
To be given away.
Everything in the photograph is on loan,
Everything borrowed,
And time running out on the debt.
What have they done today; what have they heard
To write down at night, to turn over,
To leaf through to a clear sign?
They long to be certain before the end,
Before they're borne off from the threshold
Under the stars some windy night,
Their eyes still peering ahead like this,
Straight to the thin edge of the dark.

Early Settler

You could hike to your neighbor in an hour
When you learned the short cuts. If no one was home
It was easy to hunt him up in his field.

"What brings you here?" you asked, when you met a
          stranger,
And listened to the answer all afternoon,
Sprawled on a stone, nodding at his schemes,
While your dogs whimpered futilely to be gone.

Then you told him how you loved the weather,
Sunrise and rain, green leaves and brown.
You'd hiked there for years, and learned,
Looking down from hilltops, to approve all change.

When your friend fell sick you encouraged him
To fight back. You came to the cabin with food.
You wouldn't allow a pilgrim to die young
Under your protection, held up by your right hand;
Though after a month, watching him slacken into bone,
Angry with your failure, you wished you were more
          like God.

Or maybe near the end you believed
You were really one of the gods
But had never tried hard enough,
Or were somehow losing your power.
Awful luck, you thought, for the dying man
To have chosen from hundreds the weakest one.

The Pilgrims

in memory of Wesley Kettlecamp

You were the stone heart of the high school.
On the first day your class huddled together
Trying to make sense of its bad luck.
We have been discovered, thought the guilty ones,
When they noticed you had no smiles,
No time to console us.

You were never late, and began to lecture
As you burst through the doorway, throwing off your
    coat,
Taking up your suspended thought
Mid-phrase from the last bell.
You left no gaps in the argument
For the slimmest question to squeeze through.

What other teacher ever came close to your glacier pace?
Seven full weeks on the pre-Columbian voyages
Weren't enough. You must have heard in your youth
The unabridged word on the mountain of history
From the still voice, and were under oath
To return to the valley of shadow
And repeat it all,
No holy chapter, no legend left out.

We never came close to the Revolution,
Never heard of the Civil War,
And performed shamefully on our College Aptitudes;
But none of us had the nerve to complain.
Who would tap a tide on the shoulder and ask it

To speed up? If you once were stopped
We guessed you would have to begin over.

Rumors came to us in the halls
That other classes had reached the New Deal,
Were making the world safe for democracy.
We understood we would never catch up,
Three hundred years behind with the Pilgrims,
Making the slow crossing with their fleet
On your boat to America.

Sunday

In the fading photograph of the pleasure boat
The pleasure-seekers, dressed in their Sunday best,
Crowd all three decks, women in sunhats
Pausing to chat with bearded men in derbies
Who lean on the rail, listening to the band.

On shore, the quiet farms slide by. Here and there
A cluster of low houses, a river town. The sun
Is overhead. Everyone looks willing to be interested,
Pointing to the inlets and islands, recalling their names,
Though many have boarded the boat nudged by a
        friend,
By a promise to a child, though the children are already
        lost,
Crying with their dolls in the passageways.

It's only because they're long dead
That they all look sad. But some must be happy.
Some must refuse to envy the boats in front
Or look back on the boats behind and sigh.
The ride is no empty promise to them
Of a better ride to come, and no omen of a worse.
Whatever they expected to be shown is here.

Whatever lies behind the water, the sun, the air,
The uniforms of the band, is too imperfect to be seen,
Unfinished, still composing its face in the dark,
Waiting, as this moment waited, near the surface of the
        field
Till the Sunday comes when it's ready to appear.

The End of Politics

You would be pleased to see how the latest name
Has faded from my bumper, peeled to a smear
No one can read. For you, as always,
The candidates were the same, twin shadows,
While you stared into pure light,
Some New Order slowly mapped out
On distant summer jaunts outside Milwaukee.
Now that the issues fade out
I regret my harsh words on election night,
Unreal opinions, unreal anger,
Dividing two friends who still agreed.

Evenings now, leafing through the news,
I half look for your photograph,
A few lines describing your appearance on the scene
With a modest program. Your stand
On classrooms in the factories is well received;
Your address to the grange hall is almost believed:
Let the land return to little farms,
No absentee owners,
Tractors and balers shared round
By farmers in overalls who hope for rain.
Won over by your voice, had I heard you,
I would have cheered.

A little before bed, laying aside my novel,
I go out for a stroll, nod to my neighbors

With their dogs, Democrats, Republicans.
In upstairs bedrooms, a few lights.
Any one of them, I imagine, could be yours
As you sit up late, planning your advent.
On the table your map is spread out.
Your finger hovers by the Great Lakes,
Your palm grazes the Plains.
What region of the country needs you most?
Here where your power is least expected
Would be a good place to reach out.

Today

Today keep the windows open.
Let the soul finally fly off
And preen itself in cold mountains,
Forgetting you, forgetting home.
Years spent in obedience to its small voice
And no profit, nothing for nights
With children and old men.
Lives fall out of reach and you're no wiser,
No larger than before, outdone
Even by the green shrub at the curb.

There's still time. It's not too late
For wide margins—
Whole mornings spent getting up;
A week in the shade of the porch
Sampling the wind.
Pretend you've been promised another life,
A calm wagon ride to the country
Slow enough to finish what you leave undone.

What more to hope for then but a spirit
Soaring over your roof at night,
Invited by your leisure to touch down;
A rare spirit, the one that descends only on a house
That's vacant, eases in the window
When you make no plans of your own,
Shakes out its banners in the empty room.

Independence Day

Many teachers in our country still hold jobs.
Whitman turns from the road, stands by the fence
In the big farmyard, and inspects the new corn,
No rich man's heir or slave.
And Jefferson, a little money in the bank,
A house of his own, reckons up by candlelight
In his ruled ledger cheques and balances,
Proof against cynics in the council room.

And in the woods, hiking on the weekend,
You stumble if you're lucky on a Blackfoot trail
Thinner than a handspan, fading to grass,
A curving thread at the pond's edge,
Long searched for, long explored
By the patient few in the kingdom of circles,
Summer and Winter, Spring and Fall.

Then in the city at every church corner
A smaller city rises on a hill,
A small light to the sinners.
Your brother the tinker preaches from his pew.
The Saints of the Wilderness strain to hear.
So much discomfort for a new start,
No one fat after three months,
No one alive by bread alone.

With all of them so intent on their work
You can watch them year after year unobserved.
You can stand as close as you want
And they won't look around, annoyed,
Won't ask you who you are
Or why you've come.

Contentment

I come home happy.
My students believed my lecture on progress.
The evenings are turning warm.
I'm not angry anymore that it took me so long
To enjoy my garden and welcome the sun
As its shines without judgment on the world,
Green fields and brown.

Maybe today
Even the old man in my spare room
Who never goes out
Will shuffle to the porch
And blink in the warm light.
Gently I knock at his door and step in.

There he is,
Bending at a fire in the grate,
Holding out his hands.
"Frost-bitten," he explains;
"A whole day chopping holes in the lake
And look, no fish."

"Friend," I whisper, "you've been dreaming.
You don't even need a coat today."
"Yes," he replies, "life is a dream.
I would like a few words with the dreamer
About reform. And if I'm the dreamer
What happened, I wonder, to my other dreams,

The good ones that sometimes flowed in at night,
Where I walked in the orchard with a friend?

"Now I can only come up with snow,
This meager kindling to warm my hands,
And you for drama, urging me to go."

Carpentry

Carpenters whose wives have run off
Are sometimes discovered weeping on the job.
But even then they don't complain of their work.

Whitman's father was a carpenter.
He was so happy hammering houses
That he jumped shouting from the roof beams
And rolled with a yawp in the timothy.
This led his son to conclude wrongly
That all workmen are singers.

Whitman's father was weak.
He had trouble holding a job.
He hoped that the house he was working on
Would be lived in by a wiser father
Who would earn his sleep,
Dreaming easy under a sound roof
With no rain in the face.

Of course, there are bad carpenters everywhere.
They don't care if the walls don't meet.
"After all," they argue,
"We're not building airplanes."
But Whitman's father measured his nails.
Many mornings, clacking his plane,
He crooned a song to the corners,
Urging them on to a snug fit.
Nothing that the owner values
Must escape through the cracks,
No needles of heat, no threads of light.

Morning

My right eye wakes up happy.
The sun is shining on my lashes.
From nowhere my bedroom comes back to me.
At the window I notice old women in the street
Hauling white bundles that glow with their own light.
My right eye guesses where they're heading,
Pictures how their steps interwind
As each travels her own way home
Under miles of nut trees.
Someone kind has left me this eye,
A great gift I must use more often
Till I see what the giver sees,
How the different colors of the roofs
Compose a single picture, which so far,
To my apprentice vision, has remained obscure.

Then slowly my left eye grates open,
Squinting at the vulgar sunrise,
Shading itself with the left arm.
It deserves a much handsomer room,
Thicker hair on the head in the mirror,
Deserves more respect from the world outside.
It looks down on the birds in the garden
Pecking out the life of my cherry tree.
O you greedy ones! Will you leave me nothing?
And there on his porch my left eye descries
My neighbor, whose imprisoned wife
Loves me, loves me,
Though not quite enough to break away.
At night at the window she signals gently
With gestures my right eye does not see.

The Bird Watcher

Now the coast of the country is grazed by light.
Farmers are rising in America.
Hunters in the North shoulder their guns
And march off into the woods.
The sky is crowded with small birds.
Unnoticed they scatter across fields and towns.

Now in the twilight before work
In his one moment of leisure
The bird watcher steps out of his house
To stand in the street and wait.

If a single stray circles nearby
Or calls from a maze of branches,
Or hovers as a speck far off,
The watcher, with no one nearby to look,
Points up, and with no one to listen
Breaks the silence, sounding out the name.

Masonry

for Martin Pops

The stonemason, napping after work,
Puzzles out in dream, as is right,
Conundrums of the stone trade:
Lays a brick roof on the bungalow;
Polishes a limestone clock in a kitchen
Where the cabinets are all stone.
Who knows how the hinges are fastened on?
"Bring me mortar," he mumbles from the couch
As his wife wakes him for the telephone.
A friend is calling for advice on a porch,
Something nice for a barbecue, picnics in the summer.
The mason ends up doing all the work.

Stonemasonry is the oldest trade, he explains.
All buildings begin at the northeast corner
Since Solomon ordered that his temple begin there.
Who knows why? Maybe he'd heard a rumor
That stone handled like this was gratified,
And who was he, a mere king, to deny stone?

When the mason drives in winter by a house he's built,
He imagines delicate lives inside.
Flowers must bloom in the bay window.
On the table, on grandmother's birthday,
A cake powdered with the finest sugar
Waits undisturbed for the guests.

Muggy Nights

Muggy nights too thick for sleeping
I think of you as cool in your room
A few stories above the street,
Breathing thin air from the mountains.
After hours of reading
You rest your head on the desk.
Though disappointed in the hope
Of serious friends, of serious sons,
You don't lament.
Your rest is brief,
My one friend who's given up
The crushing chore of becoming happy
And tries in the time left
Simply to be wise.

I've never found time.
Home after school,
I write letters for unschooled friends.
"Dear Linda, heavy snow is falling here.
The factories of Buffalo have shut down.
Are you free to visit me soon?
Just one of your stories would do me good."
Later, if Linda replies,
My grateful friend runs up to me on the street,
Shouting my name.

You don't hear it. You're too high up.
And later you're not disturbed

As I whistle hoarsely, passing your house,
Walking home from the late movie,
My mind on the actress with dark hair,
Dark eyes, a thoughtful smile,
Wondering what other movies she's been in,
Who in the world she reminds me of.

In the West

My mother's father missed out on Swami Muktananda.
He thought that the suits he pressed for twenty-nine
        years
In the basement of Famous–Barr Department Store
Were real, real as his skill on the French horn,
As his pride in the marches he composed for the store
        band.
The breath he blew in the horn seemed his alone,
Not part of the great wind rumored to enfold the globe,
Dropping leaves from the banks of the Ganges at his
        door.

And did the holy void lean down to listen
When his band played? He never noticed if it did.
For him the audience was his two girls,
Proud of their pa, dressed in their summer dresses
In O'Fallon Park by the gravel landing of the pond.

He never meant his weekends in his garden as a sign
That he wanted to be gathered in, plucked out of time.
The work relaxed him. It delighted his two girls,
Who hoed along with their father as a kind of play.
Maybe he thought that one day the garden
Would please their sons, and dreamed of me
At this window, gazing on the yard,
Though then, as now, in the evening light
The garden must have appeared far down
Like a garden on a card. fading at the margins,
With fainter writing on the other side.

Grandmother and I

Grandmother sits on the couch in our tiny apartment
Over the drugstore, leafing through the news.
She's larger than my parents and knows all things.
It's turning out just as she expected.
The same hoodlums are climbing on the trains
And buying up all the seats.
"You don't have to read the paper to learn this,"
She mutters to herself, and nods.

When I come to the couch and ask for a story
She bends down and whispers, slightly deaf,
"Obey your father." Her voice is warm.
Such phrases in her Russian accent often mean, "Young
      man,
How are you today, whoever you are?
Where are you going in your cowboy suit?"

We don't expect her to remember all our names.
By middle age she'd outlived five presidents
And the sons of two czars.
Napoleon himself, it's rumored, as he neared the
      border,
Stopped at Grandmother's for advice.
"You'll be sorry, Napoleon," she said;
"Go home and stay warm."
It's hard to convince an emperor.

Many have grown small with the years,
But every year Grandmother grows larger,

Like a tree by clear water.
The whole family sleeps without fear
In the widening circle of her shade.

At night in my bed,
Groping my way in dream through cloudy streets,
I hear from her branches far above
Birds that sing of the workshop of my father,
Boris the long-lost tailor, still alive,
Waiting in the story I've always loved.

III *Lost Hours*

Igor

How can I be the character I hate most
In the great novels, a Cyril or an Igor
Who visits his aging friend for a week
At Christmas, in the icy provinces,
And talks only of himself, and ignores the daughter
As she watches with clear eyes?

On departure day she hands him his coat,
Newly brushed, and looks down,
Pale and grave, rubbing her hands.

He pretends not to notice and tells lies.
"Sonia, they don't give me a moment's rest
In my job for the Czar, inspecting sheds.
Their spies have offices in the smallest towns."

Silent, she stares at the big roses
Woven in the rug, or turns to the window,
The view of the white field, the snow-bleached
Ice-hung cowfence tumbled down.

"Sonia, it's not your fondness for me,
It's your hatred for this farm—who can blame you—
That makes you long for the great world
With me as your guide, though my bad moods,
Hidden by my manners now, would spoil your fun.

"And why should a girl so young and strong
Need me to tell her every morning

If she's happy or sad, a charity case,
When now she supplies her sorrow, her joy?"

Then the coachman blows his horn.
Igor runs out, throws up his box,
Shouts something, and is off,
Wound in his scarves.
He doesn't look back.

And already it's too late. The girl's gone
And the house, and the village,
All vanished over the hills to a place
Where Igor is fiction, a paper name
Left on the seat of the carriage
When they climb out
Home.

Fiction

It's not the words of father or mother
That reach you in the night,
Beg you to get up, dress,
Follow your breath through empty streets,
Proclaiming that you're chosen.
Your parents were quiet people, modest and shy,
Who whispered to their son, "Don't fly too high,
Don't go too near the water."

You've been reading the wrong books again,
Too many children's stories of treasure
Unearthed by orphans on the beach,
By bottle boys in the ink factory,
Squatters in tar shacks by low fires.
You have a warm house, a full dinner,
Children at play with grandparents on the lawn.

These stories should be popular only in some
            underworld
Where all is given up.
There they may call in Orpheus for a song.
The hall is filled. The judges weep.
Sisyphus sits down for a moment on his stone
And dreams that his hillside is a plain,
His stone only ice, and waits for the sun.

But the sun stays up here. Orpheus hurries back
Followed by his prize, pale Euridice.

The tunnel begins to fill with faint light.
The soft sound of the beach reaches their ears.
Why at that moment does he turn around?
Why does he worry that she's having second thoughts
As images from the earth flood down?

O fool with little faith,
She was eager to come back
Even if your songs had worn off.
She was even willing to meet your parents
And would not have wept if you looked like them.

Where Have You Been?

Back then when I wore my cowboy suit to breakfast
I could find two or three at the table
In plain clothes whom I wanted to be like,
My older brothers, my father.
Even Uncle Ben, Aunt Elaine's last choice,
Had a few good features, my mother said
As she leaned at the sink, handing me plates.

There was no one in your house like that;
No father at all, and a child mother
Jealous of her children,
Choosing a different favorite every week
To unsettle the rest.
So where did you find your likeness?
Who taught you, when you left home,
To cry in your room not merely from loneliness
But from guilt, for the sisters you fought with
And left behind? Did you take your habits from a book?
What an effort to haul in pieces of yourself
From so far off, while I, yawning in the morning,
Found my cowboy suit laid out on my chair.

You tell me now how you treasure your solitude
Half out of fear that a handmade woman
Is too fragile for the world,
But I know how strong you are,
You who never wake with a jolt
In a strange bedroom,
Wondering who has brought you there.

More Light

Reading how St. Augustine said good-by in tears
To the pleasures of the world, because they wouldn't
     stay,
Because they left him starved, I took it as a sign
I should turn from you, from the ebb and flow of your
     smile,
And focus on a fixed and cold star, twinkling out of
     reach.
Now it seems I could have traveled as far from the
     world
By walking to your door, setting aside for good
My need to be blessed forever,
Trying, instead, to be satisfied for a time.
And you who used the phrase, "I've learned from you
     all I can,"
Would have learned new questions, deeper than the
     first,
To make my familiar voice again strange.
We'd have learned how to study our whole lives
And be mystified in the end,
With the meanings of all things passing us by
But skirting close, branches on the frozen lake,
A light in the burned-out house
At the edge of Bakersfield, brighter than a star.
It would have taken us twenty years to label our
     differences,
Twenty more to prove our uneasy union impossible,
To prove we could love each other elsewhere, but not
     here.

Evening Guide

If you learn to enjoy in the early evening
Eating alone, watching how the yard
Shades into purple as the edges fade,
Then you'll be free, the keys of your joy
Snug in your own pocket.
But look at you now, restless,
Half-turned in your chair,
Half-listening for the door.
You imagine that your friend is lonely somewhere;
You worry that she's not;
While the shy yard, unwooed, unobserved,
Creeps off in the dark.

If you notice how the woman who hobbles in the
        moonlight
By your house is the likeness of your aunt,
And imagine how she labors like you
To climb from her past
And become the old woman of her dreams,
Who travels every summer to another state,
Hoping to see all fifty before she dies,
Then you'll be free,
The joys of watching the stars in all skies
All yours. But look at you now,
Huddled in your chair, hunched low,
Worried that your friend enjoys the evening
Without your help.

Here is your neighbor shuffling up your drive

In the early dark, in need of advice.
Maybe his questions will inspire you.
Even your lost friend could inspire you
If you think of her waiting hours in her yard
For the night prowlers to edge out,
The shy opossum, the elusive mole,
Easing to the river for a silent drink
In the long-awaited gracious light of the moon.

Summer Night

As the moon floats over, the tin roof of the diner
Glows white. Who is left to watch it?
The customers, after supper, lumber out,
Hands in their pockets, eyes on their feet.

We'd have talked about this if you were here.
You'd have been sorry for the man who hurries to his
car.
You'd have raised the question what drags him to the
future,
What makes him believe he'll discover more wisdom
there,
More freedom than he has now,
More time for an evening stroll.

Now with you gone, he appears,
Unlocking his car, to know a secret.
It's a dark one. Others have guessed it.
And the one question he'd like to ask
Is what is taking me so long.

IV *Home and Away*

The Trip

Father and Stevie in the front seat,
Mother and Martha in the back with Grandmother
In a car going West,
Father's vacation of two weeks
Spent on the road,
Lifting the road dust in a cloud
That settles slowly as they pass.

In a town like Santa Fe
They visit the oldest house on the Continent,
Damp as a cellar, with cracked clay walls.
The children whine for ice cream.
Mother buys a postcard for a friend.
Waiting outside, Grandmother looks at the sky
And frowns. It's going to rain.

"Remember what you've seen, Children,"
Father says; "your friends will be interested.
One day you'll have your own children.
When they ask for stories
You can tell them about this."
Then he calls them to the car and drives on,
Hoping that the woman he loved years back
Was right when she told him to see the world.

Behind the motel, the children,
Excited by the early dark,

Scatter with other children on the field,
Boys chasing girls,
Girls outrunning them, shrieking
In the joy of escape, or slowing down,
All delighted by the power of their legs,
Wind on their faces, their hair.

No future tourists can be spotted here,
No writers married to their chairs,
No druggists locking their drugstores at dark,
Walking home, hunched over, in the rain.

Ashland Avenue

Even this house of ours must look like a haven
To walkers on a night like this,
When the wind, strafing the sidestreets,
Pierces the thin weave of their coats.
Half-blinded they make out our house,
Hidden in its snow shroud,
And the light leaking from shutters.
Slipping in by the side door,
They stamp off the snow in the hall.

Even when they hear us whisper,
"Why do they always show up at dinner time?
How much have they come for now?"
It must sound to their frozen ears
Like hints of welcome.
The chairs look warm, the table friendly;
And at dinner, while the shutters shake in the gale,
They eat well.
The chill of our silence, broken only by a cough
Or the scrape of a spoon on a plate,
Seems almost like a stretch of quiet
In a house where guests have come to dwell.

Everywhere

A man at home everywhere,
Isn't that what I want to be most?

Driving with no map across the plains,
I turn off the highway to rest,
Stop to buy buttons in Barkerville,
And there, ringing up change behind the counter,
Is Uncle Saul, just as I knew him years before.

"Yes, Nephew," he says,
"Barkerville is my home now.
I am happy here."

Back on the street all the families of my life
Are strolling to an open house in the neighborhood.
Through the windows I make out familiar rooms,
Familiar paintings on the walls.
These men and women are my guests.
This is where I live.

Why should I feel afraid?
What kind of a host shouts he'll be back later,
Hurries to his car,
And speeds till he's over the line?

Later I stop by a bare ridge,
Slip under a fence,
And search for a hollow I don't recognize,

Tree clumps whose markings grow vague
As I draw close.

And there in the brook, shimmering under glass,
Something I feared was the shadow of my face
Is a green leaf or a stone.

Wednesday

Who will ask in a thousand years
For houses of four walls?
They'll build new models.
The spirit will be different.
None of Buffalo's laws will survive then;
Only gravity and the howl of the dog upstairs
Left alone for the day,
And the snore of Uncle Norman napping in his chair.
The rest will have altered from within.

Already the walls are flaking.
Glancing at my watch I run outside.
I'm smitten by the look of my shadow on the lamppost
By Phelp's yellow department store in the rain
October 23rd at 3 P.M.
Where will I see it again?

But the calendar says that today is Wednesday,
Another chance held out to practice
The Wednesday talent, the Wednesday soul.
Only seven stations of the week to master,
And each the brother of those first seven
When the world was new.

Then you could leave your town,
Ramble for years a wandering road,
And always be less than a week away.

Over There

In Florence, near the Duomo, by Ghiberti's doors,
The ten gold panels, thirty years in the making,
The gems of the Baptistery, Burton adjusts his tie,
Hopeful Burton. Will Janet be herself today?
Will she wave and smile as she crosses the square?
Among the eager faces of the crowd
Burton notices that she's not there.
The play of sunlight on the bobbing hats
Is wasted here, and the slide of shadows over stones,
The glint on the low relief of the gold panels
Of Prophets and Patriarchs, as the crowd in blues,
Yellows, and reds shifts about and about
This April morning in the balmy air.
Hopeful Burton is not there. He's elsewhere,
As Ghiberti must have been elsewhere for thirty years,
Working in his studio on the doors,
Where Abraham pauses above his son,
Where the angel stretches a gold arm,
While the streets of Florence wandered by outside.

Interlude

for Mark Shechner

Coming home late, he loses his keys in the snow.
O, they will turn up in the spring thaw,
Quietly rusting side by side, still usable.
In the meantime, though, he respects the omen,
Decides it's a good time to travel.
Now, before death is prepared for,
He'll turn to a little life on the train
And slide with grace into Danville, Ohio,
In March, on the leisurely local,
And notice by the platform a barberry bush
Awaiting its new life.
Or in Jefferson, Indiana, in April,
When the train breaks down,
He'll wonder what citizens he should meet,
What wisdom Dillard and Son, Merchants,
Have found in their lumberyard.
Or else in the warm Altoona station
In May, between trains, reading a book—
Some great poem written high up
On a hilltop where the air is clear
And the smallest objects are visible—
He'll look down at himself on the bench
Reading the book by the yellow mail bags,
And be struck with the ampleness of the waiting room.

Ithaka

Happy the man who turns while old age is still green
From the cold and choppy sea to a cabin in Ithaka,
Grateful for his few sheep and pigs, and his turf walls;

Happy, when he sees how his wife has grown old,
If he guesses how her face was dried by the wind
And baked by the sun of many voyages, many returns,
As she searched for her husband's fleet, missing for
          years.

Happier still if his wife, gracious beyond hope,
Never asks what happened to his crew, her dearest
          friends,
Though maybe she still stands from habit at the
          window
In the early evening, and waits as she's always done.

In that dreamy light she looks to the happy man
Like a sad mother. Her favorite children can't get home.
Just out of sight of land, a stone's throw from the
          harbor,
They drift and founder, just far enough as they call
Not to be heard. But she hears them all.

Abraham's Dream

Mother and Father call me from their grave:
"Wait, Son. Stay in the house we left you.
Listen to the dear few you can trust."

In their hearts, though, they hanker to see the world.
Only their fear of strangers spoils things.
Mastering that, they would lead me on the road.

Meanwhile, my friends, aging, walk on.
May they all make it to the future soon.
May the future circle to my roof and rain down.

May the measures I hum at breakfast
Come from the throat of an older man,
The eyes I turn on the street be newly wrinkled,

Freshly lined. The only words I'll hear then
Will urge me in an older voice to go on,
As the dead wish when they're at their best,

And warn me not to copy from their lesser moods
An endless slower rhythm for my breath,
Breathing in one eon, breathing out the next.

The Reunion

They were only taking their summer clothes.
Why question them at the station?
Why bother to remember if they waved?
No reason at all to doubt
What they believed, that the first
Cool evening would bring them back,
Vivid with their summer news.

Is it any wonder that now, after years,
Their faces float off, jumble like dreams
And fade, try as I might every morning
To call them back? In the evening,
Walking home from the restaurant,
Turning in the alley behind the depot,
I meet Rudolph my new friend
On the run, a suitcase in each hand,
Eager to mingle with the rest,
With misty Hazel, remote Frank,
The fat man on the bus with card tricks,
The pharmacist's pale wife.
Was it she who asked to be buried in her coat
Face down, elusive to the last?

Elsewhere, no doubt, they all pile out,
All alive at once, their sleeping bags and canoes
Pulled from the bus I should be driving,
On their joyful return to camp.
Even then the noise is too loud
As they all chatter, comparing notes.
I have to make up their stories myself
And make up a listener with pencil and pad
Who writes fast enough to get them down.

Late Work

Nothing kept me home before
When the moon loomed up like this,
A great yellow face above the roof.
I would come back late, worn out,
My shoes soaked from the grass.
Now I sit dry beneath the lamp,
Trying to patch all my walks together
For my long push forward.

Somewhere inside all the sights have piled up.
Have they fallen in the right order,
Hugging like friends, blending into one?
What if each waits alone, helpless
And dumb in its small room?

The moon at the window says, "Work it out later.
I am passing over this minute.
I am always different. If you miss me now,
From this night on you begin to fade."

I keep writing as the moon passes over,
Over the dog asleep on the porch,
Dreaming of men and water,
Over the ancient dying elm,
Rooted its whole life in my yard,
Its great trunk thicker after every rain.

The Traitor

You will be the ones, my new neighbors,
You who already are idling your cars,
Bored with the scenery, restless
For an endless spin in the world,
You who cheapen my slow work, my careful lifelong
      list
Of reasons to move, still only half done,
You will be the ones when my train finally arrives,
When I'm borne to my new town,
Welcomed by trumpets, seated at the banquet by the
      mayor
Who loves me like a son,
You will be the ones they drag in bound
For snooping at the gates, with no papers, nothing to
      explain
Why you left home;
You will be the ones to beg at my chair for a sign.
"Your honor, I know these men; you can trust them,"
I will say, pale with my first lie
On my first day.

But for now I hold on here.
Winter withdraws; summer withdraws;
Another piece of my train ticket arrives.
I can almost make out the words now,
The departure time, the name in red
Of the doomed town.

The Band

Pensioners fondle the books in the sidewalk bins
For the big bargains, two for a dollar:
Eat Yourself Slim, Secret Missions of the Civil War,
Great Train Wrecks, Photographing Your Dog.
At home on their tables the books, never finished, pile
        up,
Their promises not fulfilled. The pensioners pace in
        their rooms.

Sundays they're called outside by the music of the band
From the green rotunda. The musicians strain at their
        horns.
Their necks are pinched by the starched collars of their
        uniforms.
They appear to be playing in this heat from duty,
As if asked by friends. Others may enjoy the music
If not them, so why not play for an afternoon?

The music floats up and away over the roofs
To the window of your hilltop room, where you lie in
        bed,
Whispering to your one love.
All morning you've played together slowly and quietly,
Free of the need to rush to some grand finale
That drives the strivers in the town,
The young attorneys, who crave release.

Over this ample district of the present
Floats the mournful dowdy music of the band.

It mingles with your sighs as you rise to dress.
You move with its rhythms to the straight-back chair at
      your desk
Where your paper lies ready, forms for a new agreement
Between you and the town, between the town and your
      one love

As she steps outside to mingle with the pensioners,
Who listen patiently to the band,
Hoping if they stay to the end
That something left behind in their rooms
Won't look the same when they return.

Library of Congress Cataloging in Publication Data

Dennis, Carl.
  Signs and wonders.
  (Princeton series of contemporary poets)
  I. Title.
PS3554.E535S57   811′.5′4   79-83985
ISBN 0-691-06411-3
ISBN 0-691-01363-2 pbk.